Tricky

MINDTRAP®

Puzzles

Challenge the way you think & see

DETECTIVE SHADOW

Sterling Publishing Co., Inc.

New York

Edited by Jeanette Green

Library of Congress Cataloging-in-Publication Data

Detective Shadow.
  Tricky Mindtrap puzzles: challenge the way you think and
  see / Detective Shadow.
    p. cm.
  Includes index.
  ISBN 0-8069-4488-9
  1. Lateral thinking puzzles. I. Title.
GV1507.L37 D49 2000
793.73—dc21   00-034449

10

Published by Sterling Publishing Co, Inc.
387 Park Avenue South, New York, N.Y. 10016
© 2000 by MindTrap® Games Inc.
Distributed in Canada by Sterling Publishing
c/o Canadian Manda Group, 165 Dufferin Street
Toronto, Ontario, Canada M6K 3E6
Distributed in the United Kingdom by GMC Distribution Services,
Castle Place, 166 High Street, Lewes, East Sussex, England BN7 1XU
Distributed in Australia by Capricorn Link (Australia) Pty Ltd.
P.O. Box 704, Windsor, NSW 2756, Australia
Printed in China
All rights reserved
Sterling ISBN 13: 978-0-8069-4488-3
ISBN 0–8069–4488–9
For information about custom editions, special sales, premium and
corporate purchases, please contact Sterling Special Sales
Department at 800-805-5489 or specialsales@sterlingpub.com

If you enjoy this book, please look for Detective Shadow's book,
Lateral MindTrap® Puzzles, by Sterling Publishing Co., Inc.,
which includes brainteasers, historical trivia, and murder
mysteries for you to solve. These MindTrap® puzzle books,
like the game on which they are based, will capture your
imagination and challenge the way you think.

Tricky MindTrap®

PUZZLE QUESTIONS

It will almost always contain an even number of rows—
usually twelve, fourteen, or sixteen. One with an odd
number is rarer than a four-leaf clover.

◆ How should you pronounce the second day of the week,
TEE-USE-DAY, CHOOSE-DAY, or TWOS-DEE?

■ What kind of wood-
working is done in
many offices?

● Clem Walton's father is
older than his grand-
father. How is this
possible?

> "He respects Owl, because
> you can't help respecting
> anybody who can spell
> TUESDAY, even if he doesn't
> spell it right; but spelling
> isn't everything. There are
> days when spelling TUESDAY
> simply doesn't count."
>
> A. A. Milne (1882–1956)
> *The House at Pooh Corner* (1928)

Answers on page 66.

◆ If Art Bragg's peacock laid an egg on Bertha Dribble's driveway in Chicago, Illinois, during the 1930s, who would be the rightful owner of the egg?

▨ What orchestral device is not blown, bowed, plucked, or struck?

> *"Wagner's music is better than it sounds."*
>
> Bill Nye (1850–1896)

● From statistical records, what is the most dangerous job in America?

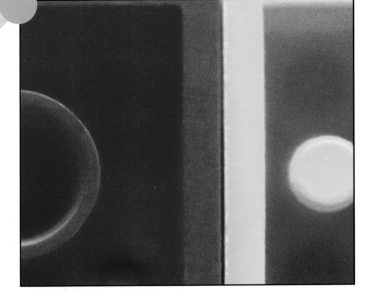

Just what two of the three little pigs needed.

Answers on page 66.

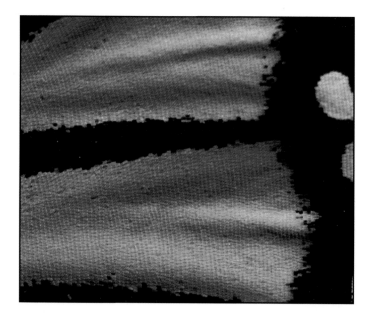

"I've crawled and I've flown. Flying's better."

◆ In what month do Americans drink the least amount of milk?

"What a waste it is to lose one's mind—or not to have a mind. How true that is."

Dan Quayle (b. 1947) *Addressing a United Negro College Fund affair and garbling their slogan "A mind is a terrible thing to waste."*

■ Many people consider it amazing that things are always in the last place you look for them. What is wrong with this belief?

● How many years did Moses wander in the desert before he entered the Promised Land?

Answers on page 67.

◆ What came first, the chicken or the egg?

"When you take the bull by the horns...what happens is a toss-up."

William Pett Ridge
(1860–1930)
Love at Paddington Green

■ If a daddy bull weighs 1,200 pounds (540 kg) and eats 12 bales of hay each day, and a baby bull, who weighs 300 pounds (135 kg), eats 4 bales of hay each day, then how much hay should a mommy bull eat if she weighs 800 pounds (360 kg)?

● What is considered by many people in the Western World to be the first transplant?

"Hey, who's picking up my tab? I'm flat broke!"

Answers on page 67.

"I'm not superstitious, I just don't like being third on the same one!"

◆ Two very popular and common objects carry out the same function, and yet one of them has thousands of moving parts and the other hasn't any. What are the two objects?

■ What are the last few hairs on a dog's tail called?

"My dog is worried about the economy because Alpo is up to almost 99 cents a can. That's almost $7.00 in dog money."

Joe Weinstein

● Of the Seven Dwarfs there were Dopey, Sneezy, Bashful, Grumpy, Happy, Sleepy, and Doc. Who was the tallest in the Seven Dwarfs' household?

Answers on page 68.

◆ If a billion follows a million and a trillion follows a billion, what number follows a trillion?

■ The 22nd and 24th presidents of the United States had the same mother and father, but were not brothers. How could this be possible?

"I don't know much about being a millionaire, but I'll bet I'd be darling at it."

Dorothy Parker
(1893–1967)

● What is it you sit in, sleep in, and brush your teeth with?

Get it together!

Answers on page 68.

If it's not rough, it'll never be smooth.

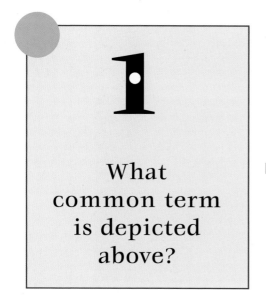

What common term is depicted above?

◆ What do both veterinarians and cat lovers usually call little cats with a white, black, red, and cream-colored coat?

■ What has four legs, a tail, eats oats and hay, and sees equally well from both ends?

Answers on page 69.

◆ What is 147 apples plus 68 oranges?

■ What is the difference between a dollar and a half and thirty five-cents?

● What do people commonly eat before it is born and after it is dead?

"Stand firm in your refusal to remain conscious during algebra. In real life, I assure you, there is no such thing as algebra."

Fran Lebowitz
Tips For Teens

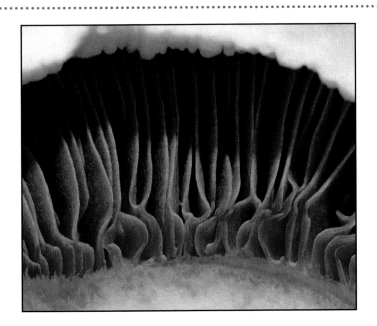

"Hey, give me a break. If you were kept in the dark and fed my diet, you'd look like this too!"

Answers on page 69.

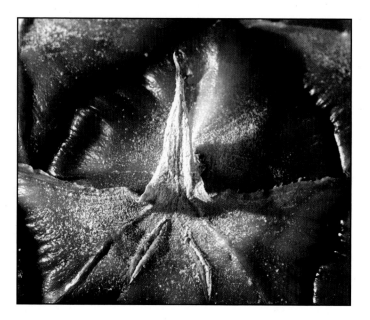

"I refuse to pine over the fact that I have two names and neither one of them is me."

◆ In the nursery rhyme "Sing a Song of Sixpence," how many bluebirds were baked in the pie?

▪ What ten-letter word beginning with "T" and ending with "R" can be typed by using only the top row of letters on a typewriter?

● What mathematical symbol can you put between 1 and 2 to make a number greater than 1 but less than 2?

Answers on page 70.

◆ Eliminate all the days of the week except for one, and to be forthright about it, this day is not the day after Sunday or the day before Wednesday, and it can't be that Saturday is tomorrow, nor can it be that Sunday was yesterday, and it most certainly couldn't be two days before yesterday, and while we're at it, let's elimate Thursday.

So, what day is it?

"Sir, Saturday morning, although recurring at regular and well-foreseen intervals, always seems to take this railway by surprise."

W. S. Gilbert (1836–1911)
Letter to the Baker Street stationmaster on the Metropolitan line

They're usually a good way to say...
whatever it is you want to say.

Answers on page 70.

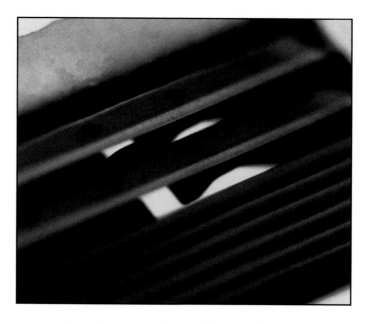

A timely cure for twilight shadows.

On the choice of color for the Model T Ford:

"Any color, so long as it's black."

Henry Ford (1863–1947)

◆ Atlantic Mutual Insurance Co. has in its New York offices one of the world's most complete collections of recorded marine disasters, mishaps, and groundings.

Although there are many famous and well-known sea adventures, which one should be listed as first?

■ Why do some people press elevator buttons with their fingers while others use their thumbs?

Answers on page 71.

◆ A deaf man, wanting to cut some wood, went to a hardware store to purchase a saw. How did he indicate to the shopkeeper that he wished to buy a saw?

If you take half of ten apples away from seven apples, what have you got?

In his old age Sir Winston Churchill (1874–1965) overheard one of two new MPs whisper to the other, "They say the old man's getting a bit past it."

"And they say the old man's getting deaf as well," said Churchill.

The tip of the iceberg it's not.

Answers on page 71.

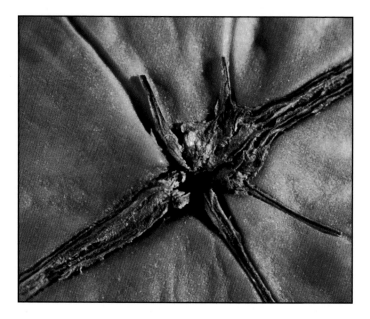

"Getting mixed up with a bunch of crazies absolutely drives me up the wall."

"If your parents never had children, chances are you won't either."

Dick Cavett

◆ President Bush has a short one. Prime Minister John Major's is bigger than Bush's. Boy George seldom uses his, and Madonna no longer has one. What is it?

■ Carry's mother had four children, not to mention a rather unhealthy fixation on monetary names. The oldest child was named Quarter. The second child was called Dimeond. The third child was named Nickelass. What was the fourth child and only girl likely named?

Answers on page 72.

◆ Don't read the words below; just say the colors they're printed in correctly in ten seconds . . . out loud.

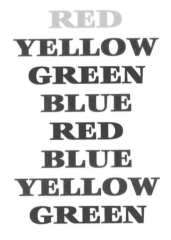

There's an even chance of being odd.

Answers on page 72.

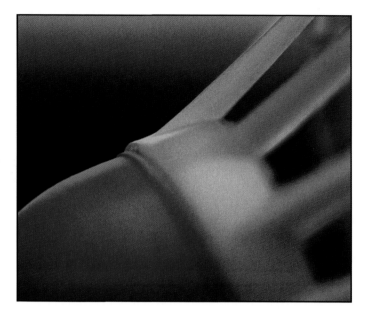

"In my younger days I had a fine cork head and
a lovely feather plume."

*"Running is an
unnatural act,
except from enemies
and to the bathroom."*

Anonymous

◆ George could see that the
finish line was near, and
with a burst of speed he
passed the others and won
the race by several feet
(2–3 meters). Although
first prize was $1,000 and a
beautiful glass trophy,
George never received
either.

Since George didn't test
"positive" for drugs and he
wasn't disqualified, why
didn't he receive the
rewards?

Answers on page 73.

◆ Many people who are interested in American history and politics, and especially Republicans, never tire of pointing out that Woodrow Wilson, a Democrat, was a character of such dubious qualities that when he ran for the presidency, his own mother didn't vote for him. Although he did win, why couldn't he have counted on his own mother's vote?

About a restaurant:
"Nobody goes there anymore. It's too crowded."

Yogi Berra (b. 1925)

Unflappable.

Answers on page 73.

The perfect part for loose lips.

◆ Art Bragg and Charles Pompuss were playing tennis on their club's only clay court. They played a total of five sets, with each of them winning three of the five sets. How was this possible?

Answers on page 74.

◆ Which of the following statements are true?

1. Exactly one of these ten statements is false.
2. Exactly two of these ten statements are false.
3. Exactly three of these ten statements are false.
4. Exactly four of these ten statements are false.
5. Exactly five of these ten statements are false.
6. Exactly six of these ten statements are false.
7. Exactly seven of these ten statements are false.
8. Exactly eight of these ten statements are false.
9. Exactly nine of these ten statements are false.
10. Exactly ten of these ten statements are false.

Metaphorically speaking, a wise person won't put them all in the same container.

Answers on page 74.

"'Long about knee-deep in June, 'bout the time they melts on the vine."

James Whitcomb Riley (1849–1916)

"I assure you that the typewriting machine, when played with expression, is not more annoying than the piano when played by a sister or near relation."

Oscar Wilde (1854–1900)

◆ Sid Shady rode into Kansas City on Thursday with several hundred dollars. Three days after his arrival, he was robbed and lost his entire fortune. Finally, broke and dejected, he left on Thursday. How was this possible?

Answers on page 75.

Parable of the Isms

Socialism: If you have two cows, you give one to your neighbor.

Communism: If you have two cows, you give them to the government, and then the government gives you some milk.

Fascism: If you have two cows, you keep the cows and give the milk to the government; then the government sells you some milk.

New Dealism: If you have two cows, you shoot one and milk the other; then you pour the milk down the drain.

Nazism: If you have two cows, the government shoots you and keeps the cows.

Capitalism: If you have two cows, you _____?

Can you fill in the blank?

"It may not be much, but it's still home."

Answers on page 75.

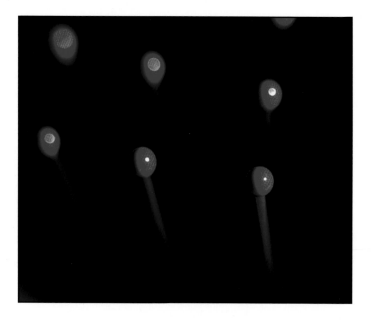

Like well-disciplined soldiers, they restore order
to an unruly world.

◆ Most American citizens have a nine-digit SSN (Social
Security number) that breaks down like this:

—The first three numbers show from what part of the
country you applied.

—The next two numbers show in coded form the year you
applied.

—The last four numbers indicate your citizen's number
kept on government file.

Given the above information, how is it possible that
since 1938, number 078–00–112 has appeared thousands
of times on individual tax returns and employers' wage
reports?

*Keep in mind that this happened long before the current convenience
of blaming every bureaucratic blunder on computer error.*

Answers on page 76.

◆ "Colonel Blackhead!" shouted General Rumple. "The Isle of Begile has a standing army of 274 of the finest soldiers in the world, but a fat lot of good it does when you can't tell me how quickly I can march them into battle! Correct me if I'm wrong, Colonel," continued the General, "but I understand that six of my soldiers can walk one-sixth of a mile in 6 minutes—is that correct?"

"Why, yes it is," replied Blackhead.

"Fine!" shouted Rumple. "So tell me then, how many soldiers will it take to march 10 miles in 6 hours?"

What answer would you give to General Rumple?

Night light.

Answers on page 76.

At least there's no jet lag on this flight.

◆ Professor Quantum loved to tell his nephew and nieces bedtime stories from memory. What puzzled Quantum was how quickly the children fell asleep. What nursery rhyme was Quantum telling?

> *"Many years ago, a small number of child laborers were attempting to traverse a more elevated position in a vain attempt to procure a quarter of a rundlet of a hydrogen and oxygen compound. Half their number experienced an uncontrollable descent that resulted in severe damage to the pate. And it soon came to pass that the rest of the labor force followed suit but with far less serious consequences."*

Answers on page 77.

◆ Dee Septor, the world-famous magician, claimed that given the right wind conditions, he could travel from the United States to Russia in a hot-air balloon in less than 2 hours. How could Dee Septor manage this feat—or could he?

> *"Fall is my favorite season in Los Angeles, watching the birds change color and fall from the trees."*
>
> David Letterman

■ Thirty birds sit on the upper branches of a tree. If a hunter fires a volley of buckshot and kills one-half of two-thirds of them, how many birds would be left?

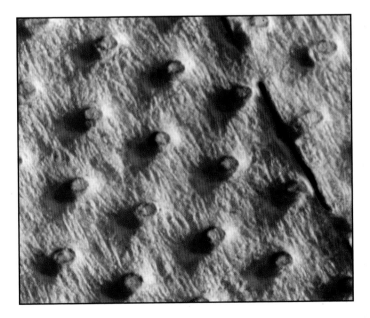

The wetter it gets, the more it dries.

Answers on page 77.

Just for the record, let's wind it up.

Formula for success:

"Rise early, work hard, strike oil."

J. Paul Getty (1892–1976)

◆ Prior to 1936, the economy of Saudi Arabia depended on two things: tourism (to Mecca and Medina) and the export of dates. Following the discovery of oil and its refinement, the country began to tap its immense wealth. In spite of having over 25% of the world's known petroleum reserves, Saudi Arabia still imports almost $1 billion of oil each year. Why?

Answers on page 78.

◆ Art Conn, Gloria Goody, and Dr. Prod were staying at the Soul-Ace Hotel on the Isle of Begile, where the natives always lie and the visitors always tell the truth. While sitting on one of the hotel's balconies overlooking the crashing waves of Perjurers' Cove, Gloria turned to Art and said, "Art, I think you're a liar."

Art looked into Gloria's eyes and replied, "Me? I don't think so. It's Dr. Prod here who's the liar."

Dr. Prod, not being one to take accusations lightly, interjected, "As far as I'm concerned, you're both liars!" And with that Prod stomped off in a huff.

Since two of the three are lying, who is telling the truth?

Cool it!

Answers on page 78.

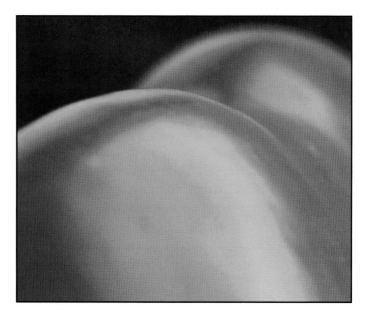

Some like 'em hot!

"I had a boring office job. I cleaned the windows in the envelopes."

Rita Rudner

◆ It is well-known that the hearty emperor penguin lives in the subzero temperatures of the Antarctic. Ironically, however, when these penguins are imported to zoos in the temperate regions, they often catch cold and die. Why?

Answers on page 79.

◆ A child is born in Boston, Massachusetts, to parents who were both born in Boston, Massachusetts. This child is not an American citizen. How could this be possible?

"The opposite of talking isn't listening. The opposite of talking is waiting."

Fran Lebowitz

"The trouble with eating Italian food is that five or six days later you're hungry again."

George Miller

Answers on page 79.

"Hey, loosen up!"

◆ Art Bragg often boasted that he never required anyone's help for anything. Then one day it all changed. Both Art and his wife had to ask someone to help them do something that they couldn't do themselves. The person they chose was their next-door neighbor, Reggie. Not only was Reggie 83 years old, but he was also deaf and confined to a wheelchair. Nevertheless, Reggie wheeled over to the Braggs' and provided assistance that neither Art nor his wife could do on his or her own. Since Reggie didn't possess any particular skill or talent, what could he have been asked to do?

Answers on page 80.

◆ After basic communication, we are taught colors and shapes. For example, the shape of a six-sided surface would be a cube. That being the case, can you correctly identify at least three of the following? A three-dimensional shape that has no more than:

A. one surface?

B. two surfaces?

C. three surfaces?

D. four surfaces?

E. five surfaces?

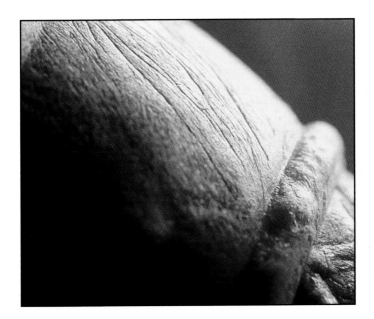

An edible handle.

Answers on page 80.

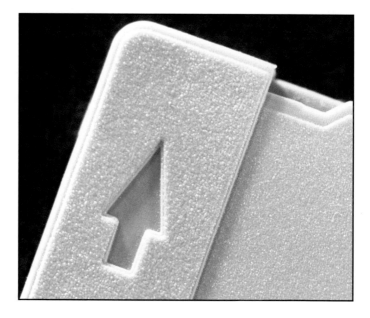

"I don't mean to brag, but I do have a rather magnetic personality."

"My niece was in The Glass Menagerie at school. They used Tupperware."

Cathy Ladman

◆ Clem Walton was born and raised in the Tennessee hills. As a young boy, unsure of his real roots, he left home with only a knapsack and an identity crisis. Clem was on a search for both buffalo and himself. Failing miserably in both quests, Clem returned to discover his roots at a family reunion. At the party he was greeted by his mother's only sister's husband's sister-in-law. Since the husband had no brothers, what relationship did this woman have to Clem?

Answers on page 81.

◆ When the third-grade teacher was asking her students to recall some of their favorite bedtime stories, boy-genius Theory Quantum immediately volunteered. "I can't remember it word for word," said Theory, "but I believe it goes something like this:

> "Ahoy, jiggle, jiggle! Yonder cavorts a *Felis domestica* with both a catgut and bow, while quite incredibly a *Bos Taurus* curveted the luminous globe, causing the diminutive *Canis familiaris* to cachinnate such a diversion while the trencher eloped with a ladle."

What rhyme was Theory recalling?

"Currently, I'm not doing anything."

Answers on page 81.

Dam the flow.

◆ Professor Quantum was nearing the end of his lecture on the American Agricultural Revolution when he realized his voice was in keen competition with a rather sleepy, snoring Hilda Frump. Professor Quantum, who savored these opportunities like a fine wine, leaned over and asked Hilda what key event occurred on November 31, 1793, that sparked the beginning of the Agricultural Revolution.

    Fortunately for Hilda, she woke up just in time to hear most of the question and responded by saying that it had to be the invention of the cotton gin by Eli Whitney. Is Hilda's answer correct, and if not, why not?

Answers on page 82.

◆ In 1969 Pan American Airlines accepted over 80,000 reservations for commercial flights, but failed to specify either the dates or times of the trip(s). Furthermore, to this day, they have not bothered to honor a single reservation. Ironically, they haven't received any formal complaints. Why not?

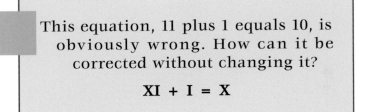

This equation, 11 plus 1 equals 10, is obviously wrong. How can it be corrected without changing it?

XI + I = X

Cell mates.

Answers on page 82.

Prior to its invention in the 1850s, British soldiers used bayonets, pocket knives, or, all else failing, rifle fire.

"A tourist is a fellow who drives thousands of miles so he can be photographed standing in front of his car."

Emile Ganest

◆ Ironically, more is known about some of the pre-Egyptian civilizations than about the early Egyptian civilizations. This is said to have happened because of an invention by the early Egyptians. What could they have invented that has deprived modern people of their storied past?

Answers on page 83.

◆ In the string of letters below, can you cross out all the unnecessary letters so that a logical sentence remains?

ALALTLH

ALALTLHOEGUICNANL

ESCEENSTSEANRCYEL

REETMTAEIRSNS

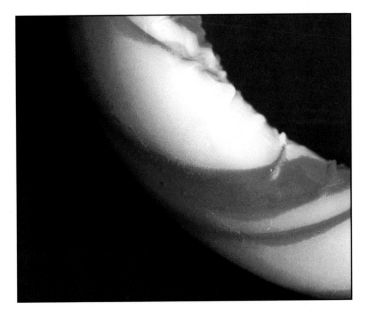

I wouldn't advise leaning on it.

Answers on page 83.

"I'm just a small cog in a much bigger wheel."

"Once upon a time there was this ovum, consisting of an envelope of albumen, jelly, and membranes, that decided to moor its entirety on a parapet. Then rather suddenly, and without notice, the ovular being succumbed to a Brobdingnagian gravitational pull. The result was that the entire embodiment of the paramount's yeomanry and herbivores were unequal to the task of assemblage."

◆ Professor Quantum was telling his young nephew Theory a bedtime story that he himself had enjoyed as a young boy. Unfortunately for Theory, Quantum recalled this popular nursery rhyme from memory—which means it was told in the professor's own words. What rhyme was it?

Answers on page 84.

◆ The island of Aruba is well-known for its beaches and perfectly predictable warm, sunny weather. In fact, Aruba's weather is so predictable that the daily newspapers don't even bother to print a forecast. Strangely enough, however, one New Year's Eve as the islanders were counting down the last 10 seconds of 1988, it began to rain. Since this occurrence is so rare, what are the chances from 1% to 100% that 72 hours later the sun will be shining?

"Rowe's Rule: the odds are 5 to 6 that the light at the end of the tunnel is the headlight of an oncoming train."

Paul Dickson

"You know it is not a good wax museum when there are wicks coming out of people's heads."

Rick Reynolds

Answers on page 84.

"There are no diamonds in my tips;
I'm just the poor little relative."

*"When I was a boy
I was told that any-
body could become
President; I'm begin-
ning to believe it."*

Clarence Darrow
(1857–1938)

◆ Octavius was born in Rome on the last day of 11 B.C. Let's suppose that in those days he had to be 16 years of age before he could obtain a learner's permit for a chariot's license. Since Octavius waited 2 days after his sixteenth birthday before applying for his permit, in what year did he apply?

Answers on page 85.

◆ Theory Quantum loved to be read bedtime stories, but unfortunately his uncle, Professor Quantum, had misplaced his glasses. Not to be discouraged, Theory suggested he tell him one from memory. The professor retold this nursery rhyme as accurately as he could remember. Which one was it?

"A Lilliputian female who was an unmarried *Homo sapiens* seedling decided to moor herself on a bit of volcanic detritus in order to gormandize on casein and other forms of coagulation. The next cognitive realization she had was when an arachnid arbitrarily decided to settle on the same volcanic detritus, resulting in her terrorized withdrawal."

"Okay, I'll bite. What is it?"

Answers on page 85.

"My husband thinks that health food is anything you eat before the expiration date."

Rita Rudner

"The guy who invented the first wheel was an idiot. The guy who invented the other three, he was a genius."

Sid Caesar

◆ The Massachusetts Institute of Technology has come up with a new method for replenishing this natural resource. It was traditionally done by hand, but this method is now considered too labor-intensive and therefore too expensive. The Institute's suggestion is to encase each one in a cone-shaped biodegradable container, and bomb a particular area. What would they be doing?

Answers on page 86.

◆ When the Isle of Begile took their most recent census, they were quite surprised to find that their population had swelled to 100,002 people. Since nobody on the Isle has more that 100,001 hairs on his or her head, what is the probability that at least two of these heads have exactly the same number of hairs?

▢ Following the Red Scare during the 1950s and 1960s, the F.B.I. (U.S. Federal Bureau of Investigation) became the largest financial contributor to the American Communist party. Why?

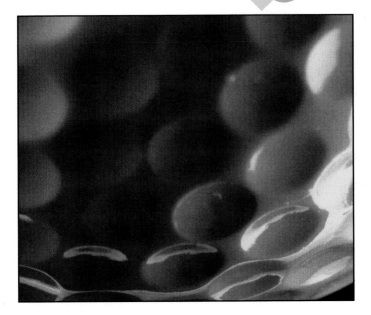

No driver's license required.

Answers on page 86.

"Neat as a pin" and "Bob's your uncle."

◆ Sam Slug was halfway across the bridge when he heard a loud bang. The car veered toward the railing as Sam fought to keep it under control. Easing the car to a stop, Sam and Sid Shady got out to see that their front tire was blown.

Knowing Constable Bumlinger was only minutes behind, Sam raced to get the spare while Sid frantically jacked up the car. Sid cranked furiously to loosen the stubborn lug nuts while Sam muttered for him to hurry. Sid finally got the last nut off and threw it in the hubcap with the others. Sam hoisted the spare into place.

Just as Sam got it on, he stepped back to straighten up, and accidentally kicked the hubcap, spilling the lug nuts into the water below. Just about then, the faint sound of Bumlinger's siren could be heard in the distance. It was still almost a mile to the border. How could Sid and Sam get away?

Answers on page 87.

◆ At 9 A.M. on a Tuesday, Bertha Dribble and the 300-car locomotive she was operating approached the intersection of Isle Rail and Begile Road at 62 miles (100 km) per hour.

At the same time, a 300-horsepower pickup truck with no brakes, no horn, and no headlights was also approaching the same intersection at 62 miles (100 km) per hour.

Several seconds later, both the train and the truck went through the intersection without colliding. How was this possible?

> *"When two trains approach each other at a crossing, they shall both come to a full stop and neither shall start up until the other has gone."*
>
> A law in Kansas

Get a handle on it; otherwise you may be under it.

Answers on page 87.

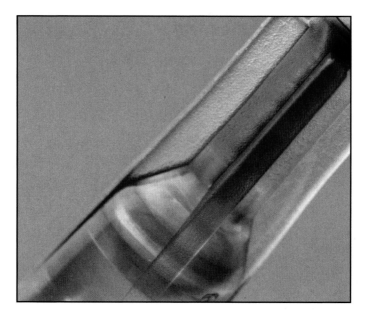

"Hey I'm serious, you really get under my skin!"

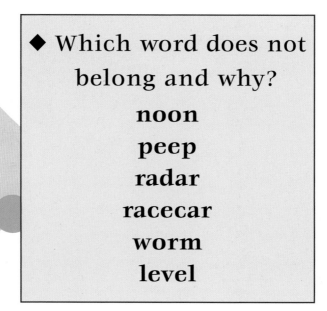

◆ Which word does not belong and why?

noon

peep

radar

racecar

worm

level

Answers on page 88.

◆ "Packed as tight as sardines" is a common metaphor used by speakers and writers alike. Why would a manufacturer who sells sardines packed in oil try to squeeze so many fish into each can?

■ Why is it that in very old homes, glass is often thicker at the bottom of windowpanes than at the top?

A child explaining the harmful effects of oil on sea life:

"When my mum opened a tin of sardines last night it was full of oil and all the sardines were dead."

Vincent Shanley &
John Golds
Classroom Changers

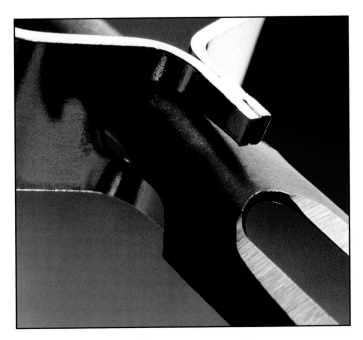

"Peel me a grape."

Answers on page 88.

Shopping tip:
"You can get shoes for 85 cents at bowling alleys."

Al Clethen

In 1768, a missionary was captured in the jungle by a tribe of cannibals. Once bound to a stake, the missionary began to preach like he had never preached before. Surprisingly, his sermon had an effect. The tribe found him so unpalatable, they decided not to eat him.

They did, however, condemn him to death, and to be extra nice, they decided to give him one of three choices. He could choose to be burned at the stake, thrown into a pit of lions who hadn't eaten in 2 years, or boiled in oil.

Which choice would give him the best chance of survival, or wouldn't it make any difference?

Answers on page 89.

◆ It is the most efficient form of motion known to science. It surpasses all other machines and animals from planes to trains to cheetahs and eagles. In transporting a quantity of weight across a given distance, this form of movement uses less energy than any other. What is it?

Caption for cartoon "The Dejected Rooster":

"What's the use? Yesterday an egg, tomorrow a feather duster."

Mark Fenderson (1873–1944)

■ Eggs, with few exceptions, are slightly narrower at one end. What useful purpose does this serve?

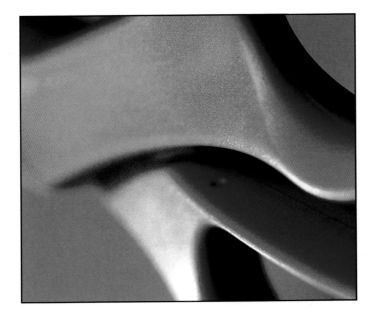

They were brought together by sheer force.

Answers on page 89.

Paper's nail.

◆ Although this scenario isn't possible, suppose you were able to take an ordinary sheet of paper and tear it into two equal-size pieces. Then you stack these two halves together and tear them in half (giving you four pieces), then you stack the four pieces together and tear them in half (giving you eight pieces), and so on until you've done this 52 times. Approximately how high would this pile rise? *Note: 500 sheets equal about 2 inches (5 cm).*

A. between 10 feet and 100 feet (3.3 to 33 m)
B. between 100 feet and 1,000 feet (33 to 330 m)
C. between 1,000 feet and 1 mile (330 m and 1.6 km)
D. between 1 mile and 10 miles (1.6 km and 16 km)
E. between 10 miles and 10,000 miles (16 km and 160,000 km)
F. well beyond 10,000 miles (160,000 km)

Answers on page 90.

◆ Clement L. Wragge, a 19th century Australian weatherman, is credited with being the first person to name cyclonic storms. He chose biblical names, such as Rakem, Sacar, Talman, and Uphaz. Following World War II, however, the World Meteorological Service also began giving names to all major storms. Why?

"You can't turn a thing upside down if there's no theory about it being the right way up."

G. K. Chesterton
(1874–1936)

▪ If today is Sunday, what is the day that follows the day that comes after the day that precedes the day before yesterday?

"I'm hooked on this stuff."

Answers on page 90.

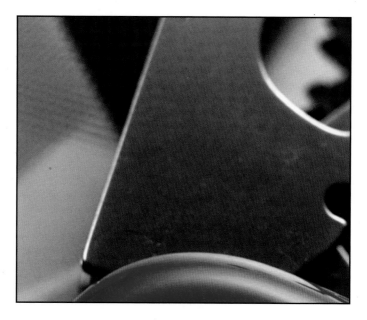

The world's smallest toolbox.

Samuel Goldwyn (1882–1974), talking about his film The Secret Life of Walter Mitty *(1947) with story author James Thurber (1894–1961) said, "I hope you didn't think it was too blood and thirsty." Thurber replied, "Not only did I think so, but I was horror and struck."*

◆ Detective Shadow responded to a 911 which brought him to Sam Slug's annual family reunion bash. To call it a bash was appropriate, since the Slug family wouldn't consider it to be much of a party if, at the very least, the police weren't called to put a stop to the festivities. This particular family reunion rapidly turned into a brawl when Grandma Slug hauled off and decked the only sister-in-law of the sister of Sam's father.

Which relative of Sam's did Grandma Slug sucker punch?

Answers on page 91.

◆ Professor Quantum never tired of reminding his Middle Eastern students that the greatest gift modern man received from the Arabs was nothing. What could he mean?

■ Barney Dribble had exactly $5,600 saved to buy a pre-owned (used) taxicab. The cab he had in mind cost $5,000 and came with a 15,000-mile (24,000-km) bumper-to-bumper warranty, except it hadn't any tires. Barney found tires at a cost of $100 each that came with a 10,000-mile (16,000-km) warranty. How could Barney drive 15,000 miles (24,000 km) under full warranty without exceeding his budget?

"Yellow is definitely my color."

Answers on page 91.

"Hey, don't pick on me, I'm just doing my job."

◆ Art Conn was the most ruthless efficiency expert on the Isle of Begile. When a business needed to cut costs and improve the bottom line, Art got the call. Art approached the receptionist of the Dollar Daze Department Stores and introduced himself. "Oh yes, Mr. Conn," she replied, "go on into the boardroom; they're expecting you."

"Mr. Conn," greeted the CEO, "I was just suggesting that we begin awarding $25 for any money-saving ideas that our employees submit. Since you haven't had time to examine our company you won't be able to participate, but it might be fun for you to sit in anyway."

"Oh, not at all," replied Art, "I think I can make a suggestion right now and be first to claim the $25."

Since Art had not yet acquired any working knowledge of the company, what did he suggest?

Answers on page 92.

◆ In 1991, Dimitrius, the old Greek historian, celebrated his 65th birthday. Realizing that he wasn't getting any younger and desperately wanting to see the great old pyramids and other relics first-hand, he decided to reward himself with a trip to Egypt for his 70th birthday.

Five years later to the day, Dimitrius stood before the great pyramids of Egypt. Noticing the names of other tourists inscribed in the stones, he took out a small knife and etched his name with the others. This occurred in 1986. How was this date possible?

"Of course I'm shaken—my sidekick's not around."

Answers on page 92.

◆ Ned Harper was the requisitions officer for a Midwestern college. Early in his post at the college, Ned realized that he had to phrase certain requests for money in a certain way or the college administrators would flatly reject them. On one occasion, the Statistics Department of the college asked Ned to supply them with some rather common and simple items.

Ned filled out the required paperwork and requested funds to buy "multiple sets of random number generators." The college administrators granted his request. What was he asking for?

■ Adult blue whales have been found that weigh in excess of 150 tons (135 metric tons). During the heyday of whaling, as many as 30,000 whales were harvested annually. The entire whale was so valuable that virtually all parts were used. The skin was used for leather, the cartilage for glue, and the blubber for lamp fuel, lubricants, oils, and cosmetics.

If the normal weight of an adult big blue is 120 tons (108 metric tons), and the liver generally accounts for 3% of its total weight, on average how many pounds (or kilograms) of cod liver oil could a whaler expect to extract?

Answers on page 93.

◆ If a successful career in the record industry is measured by the number of times people listen to an artist's recordings, then Jane Barbe is likely the most successful recording artist of all time.

Incredibly, however, very few people outside of her immediate circle of family, friends, and business associates would link her name with her voice.

Why not?

"I have made this [letter] longer than usual, only because I have not had the time to make it shorter."

Blaise Pascal (1623–1662)
Letters Provinciales (1657)

■ At the Business Computers annual ball, conversations competed with the whining sound of the blues.

"So, John, you're a vice president of IBM. What do you think of Henry gettin' his new position?" shouted Alan, the head of development with Computer Links. "I mean, here's this guy who got the top job, with all the prestige and money to go with it, for no other reason than who his bloody parents are."

"I think it's ridiculous," agreed John. "I mean really, I know for a fact he can't read or write to save his soul and he certainly hasn't put in an honest day's work in his whole life! If anyone should have gotten the job, it should have been his sister!"

In what situation could such an incapable person be granted the top position?

Answers on page 93.

◆ Dee Septor, the world-famous magician, always insisted on purchasing his own stage props and other tricks of his trade. After shopping all day, Dee arrived home and began to check his purchases against his list.

Strangely enough, Dee emptied several large containers and actually found that two of them weighed less when they were full than they did empty. How was this possible?

> *"All the fun's in how you say a thing."*
>
> Robert Frost (1874–1963)

■ Centuries ago, dueling was a common way to resolve disagreements. A proper duel required two participants and a referee. In one noted instance, Art Bragg and Dr. Prod were drinking lemonade when they discovered that they were dating the same girl. The inevitable ensued: a duel at dawn. The next morning the referee instructed them to start back to back, march off 20 paces, turn, and, facing in opposite directions, begin the sword fight.

Since Bragg and Prod had both lost their nerve from the night before, they each tried to wangle their way out while saving face. To this end they insisted the referee's rules were crazy, since it wouldn't be possible to duel facing opposite directions. What exactly is wrong with the referee's instructions?

Answers on page 94.

◆ Sam Slug approached the desk and gave his name to the receptionist. "Ah yes, Mr. Slug, we've been expecting you," the receptionist said. "Have a seat and help yourself to a cookie." "Don't mind if I do," replied Sam, filling his pockets. Several minutes later Sam was called in to an adjacent room, and just as he entered he realized they had been waiting for him.

The last thing Sam could remember was being stabbed by a man in a mask and seeing his blood squirt from the wound. When Sam eventually regained consciousness he found that his wound had been bandaged and that he was able to walk. Happy to be alive, Sam quickly left without bothering to report the incident to anyone. Why not?

■ Beulah marched over to the three eligible bachelors trying their best to look inconspicuous. "I wanna dance, so which one of you's is the best dancer?!"

"It certainly isn't me," said Art Bragg as quickly as he could. "It's definitely Barney Dribble," offered Sam Sham. "Sam Sham's lying," countered Barney Dribble.

Since Beulah knew that only one of the answers was true, and the other two were lying, who did she yank onto the dance floor?

> *"'Contrariwise,'
> continued Tweedledee,
> 'if it was so, it
> might be; and if it
> were so, it would be:
> but as it isn't, it
> ain't. That's logic.'"*
>
> Lewis Carroll
> (1832–1898)
> *Through the
> Looking-Glass (1872)*

Answers on page 94.

◆ This riddle has tricked mathematicians for centuries.

> *On my way to the fair,*
> *I met seven jugglers and a bear.*
> *Every juggler had three cats,*
> *Every cat had three rats,*
> *Every rat had two mice,*
> *All the mice had nine lice,*
> *Lice, mice, rats, and cats,*
> *Seven jugglers and a bear,*
> *How many in all were going to the fair?*

■ Below are all the letters of the alphabet with the exception of the letter "Z". Each of these letters has been placed either above or below the line for a particular reason. In keeping with this reasoning, where would the "Z" (pronounced ZEE) go and why?

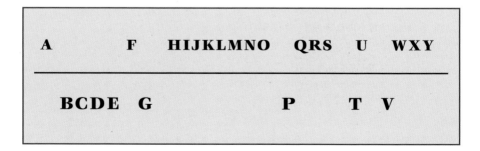

A   F   HIJKLMNO   QRS   U   WXY

——————————————————————————

BCDE G   P   T   V

Answers on page 95.

◆ Mr. Greenwich and his wife, Ms. Greenwich, were shopping when they decided to go their separate ways to speed things up. They agreed to meet at the bank at 2:00 P.M.

Mr. Greenwich realized several minutes later that he had forgotten his watch. He asked a lady walking by for the correct time. Her watch was 5 minutes fast, but she thought it was 10 minutes slow.

Ms. Greenwich had forgotten her watch, so she asked a gentleman who was passing by the correct time. The man's watch was 10 minutes slow, but he thought it was 15 minutes fast.

Taking into account the errors in the watches, who was at the bank first and at what time did each arrive?

■ What is this riddle poem about?

> Often talked of, never seen,
> Ever coming, never been,
> Daily looked for, never here,
> Still approaching, coming near.
> Thousands for its visit wait,
> But alas for their fate,
> Tho' they expect me to appear,
> They will never find me here.

Answers on page 95.

◆ A man and a boy who are walking together step out with the right foot first. The boy walks three paces while the man walks two. When will they both put the left foot forward together? Explain.

■ Here's another riddle.

> Forward I'm heavy, backwards I'm not.
> What am I?

No Comment

"We try to anticipate some of your questions so that I can respond 'No comment!' with some degree of knowledge..."

Political spokesperson reportedly responding to a group of journalists

Answers on page 95.

Tricky MindTrap®
Puzzle Answers

Corn-on-the-cob

◆ It should be pronounced MONDAY.

■ We know it as pencil sharpening.

● Clem's father is older than Clem's *maternal* grandfather.

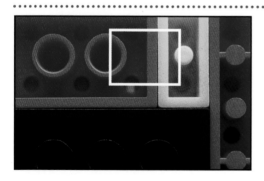

Lego blocks

◆ Peacocks cannot lay eggs. This ability belongs to the peahen.

■ The conductor's baton.

● President. Four U.S. presidents out of 42 have been assassinated: Abraham Lincoln, James Garfield, William McKinley, and John F. Kennedy.

Answers for puzzles on pages 6-7

Butterfly

◆ In February, since it has the least number of days.

▪ It would be more amazing if they were not. Once you find something, you don't look elsewhere.

● Moses reached the Promised Land. However, God forbade him entrance.

Tab on soda-pop can

◆ The egg came first. Dinosaurs were laying eggs millions of years before the first chicken evolved.

▪ There's no such thing as a mommy bull.

● Adam's rib.

Book of matches

◆ An hourglass and a sundial.

■ Dog hairs.

● Snow White, of course, was the tallest.

Zipper

◆ One trillion and one.

■ They were the same person. Grover Cleveland (1837–1908) served two terms as president, but the terms were not consecutive. He was president from 1885 to 1889 and from 1893 to 1897.

● A chair, a bed, and a toothbrush.

Answers for puzzles on pages 10–11

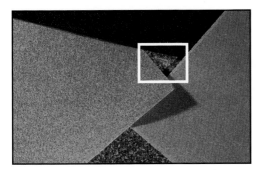

Sandpaper

◆ They call them kittens.

▨ It's a hole in one.

● A blind horse.

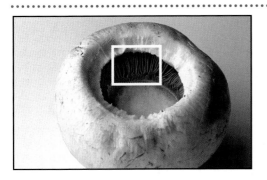

Mushroom cap

◆ It's either a lot of fruit or 147 apples plus 68 oranges....
You cannot add apples and oranges; after all, apples are
apples and oranges are oranges.

▨ None. A dollar and a half is the same as thirty five-cents
but definitely not the same as thirty-five cents.

● A chicken.

Pineapple

◆ None. They were blackbirds.

> Sing a song of sixpence,
> A pocket full of rye,
> Four and twenty blackbirds
> Baked in a pie.

■ The word is TYPEWRITER.

● A decimal point.

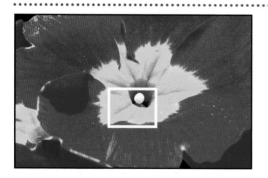

Flower

◆ Saturday.

> *"Cats are smarter
> than dogs. You can't
> get eight cats to pull
> a sled through snow."*
>
> Jeff Valdez

Answers for puzzles on pages 14–15

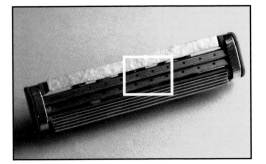

Razor blade

Noah's Ark

"Built in 2448 B.C. Gopher wood, pitched within and without. Length, 300 cubits; width, 50 cubits; height, 30 cubits. Three decks. Cattle carrier. Owner: Noah and Sons. Last reported stranded on Mount Ararat."

◆ Noah's Ark. When someone inquired about the first marine mishap Atlantic Mutual had on file, they replied with this note (see box):

▪ So that the elevator will move.

Asparagus tip

◆ He said to the shopkeeper, "I would like to buy a saw, please."

▪ Five apples. It's true that two are left, but you've still got half of ten.

Walnut

◆ A last name.

■ She named the girl Carry.

> *"A portrait is a picture in which there is something wrong with the mouth."*
>
> Eugene Speicher
> (1883–1962)

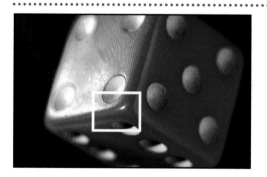

Die (the plural is *dice*)

◆ If you managed to say the correct colors in 10 seconds, congratulations!

Badminton shuttlecock, or birdie

◆ George is a horse.

Feathers or wing

◆ She couldn't. American women didn't have the right to vote before 1920.

> *"'There's no use trying,' she said. 'One can't believe impossible things.' 'I daresay you haven't had much practice,' said the Queen. 'When I was your age, I always did it for half-an-hour a day. Why, sometimes I've believed as many as six impossible things before breakfast.'"*
>
> Lewis Carroll (1832–1898)
> *Alice's Adventures in Wonderland* (1865)

Button

◆ They were partners playing doubles. The team of Art and Charles won three sets and the other team won two sets.

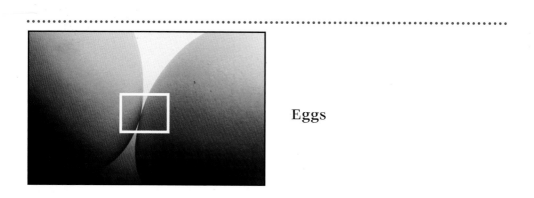

Eggs

◆ Statement #9. Since each of the ten statements contradicts the other nine, only one of them can be correct. It just happens that statement #9 correctly accuses the other nine statements of being false.

Answers for puzzles on pages 22–23

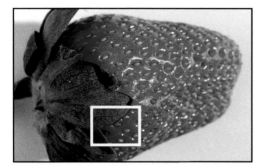

Strawberry

◆ *Thursday* was the name of his horse.

> *"If three-fourths of the Earth's surface is covered with water, how come it's so hard to get to the beach?"*
>
> Teressa Skelton

Seashells

◆ ...sell one and buy a bull.

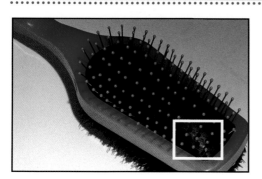

Hairbrush

◆ It was a sample number used by a wallet manufacturer to demonstrate how cards of this size would fit. Although the sample card was marked "specimen," many people who bought the wallets assumed this sample number to be their own personal SSN. As Murphy's Law would have it, it took over 20 years to straighten out most of the mess.

Note: The sample has only 8 and not the usual 9 numbers.

Bicycle reflector

◆ "I dunno, sir! The number of soldiers marching has no bearing on the speed they can march."

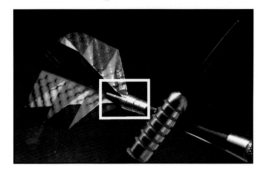

Dart

Jack and Jill
Went up the hill
To fetch a pail of water;
Jack fell down
And broke his crown
And Jill came tumbling after.

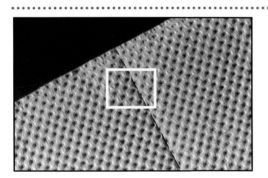

Paper towel

◆ It's no great feat if attempted in the right location. Big Diomede Island (Russia) and Little Diomede Island (United States) lie less than 3 miles (4.8 km) apart in the middle of the Bering Strait. Since the strait is frozen from October to June, one could easily walk the distance in less than 2 hours.

■ None. No bird would stay after the first shot.

Answers for puzzles on pages 28–29

Audio cassette tape

◆ Saudi Arabia imports almost $1 billion of cooking oil. You can't cook with petroleum.

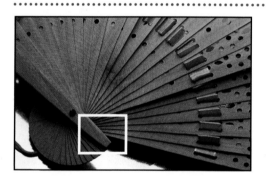

Wooden fan

◆ Art Conn. Since only one of them can be telling the truth, it stands to reason that Gloria's statement must be false. If Gloria's statement (about Art's being a liar) were true, then Art's statement about Dr. Prod's being a liar would be false, making Dr. Prod a truth-teller—which cannot be, since there is only one truth-teller.

Therefore, we know that Gloria is definitely lying and is therefore a native. If Dr. Prod's statement were true, it would mean that Gloria's statement about Art's being a liar would be false, making Art a truth-teller. The key to understanding Dr. Prod's statement is to realize that it is only partially true. When he says they're both liars, in actuality one of them is and one of them isn't, which makes the statement false. Right?

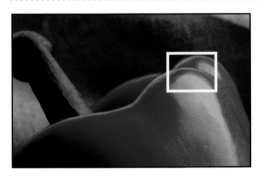

Red pepper

◆ The Antarctic is so cold it's practically antiseptic, which means the emperor penguins haven't built up immunities to many common germs.

Spaghetti

◆ The child was born before 1776, the year of the American Declaration of Independence, and is therefore a British subject.

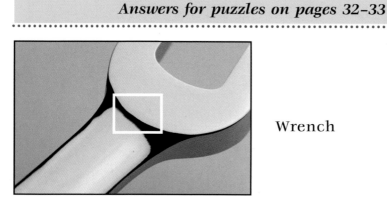

Wrench

◆ Reggie was asked to witness the Braggs' signature on a legal document.

Ice-cream cone

◆ A. A one-surface shape is a ball.
B. A two-surface shape is a cone.
C. A three-surface shape is a cylinder.
D. A four-surface shape is a three-sided pyramid.
E. A five-surface shape is a four-sided pyramid.

Computer floppy disk

◆ The woman who greeted him was his mother.

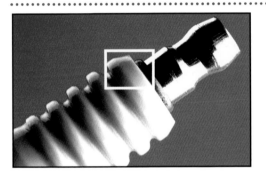

Spark plug

High diddle diddle,
The cat and the fiddle,
The cow jumped over the moon;
The little dog laughed
To see such sport,
And the dish ran away with the spoon.

Answers for puzzles on pages 36–37

Bandages

◆ Her answer couldn't be correct—November has only 30 days.

Batteries

◆ They don't fly there. Pan American Airlines began accepting reservations for commercial flights to the moon after the first moonwalk. Subsequently, they received over 80,000 requests for commercial flights destined for the moon.

■ Turn the card upside down. Now it reads: 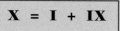 or 10 equals 1 plus 9.

Can opener

◆ Papyrus, the forerunner of paper, which unfortunately rots with age. The earlier civilizations kept their records on stone tablets, which for the most part have survived the ages.

Candy cane

◆ Cross out all the letters that spell:

"ALL THE UNNECESSARY LETTERS"

Then the remaining letters will spell:

"A LOGICAL SENTENCE REMAINS."

Answers for puzzles on pages 40–41

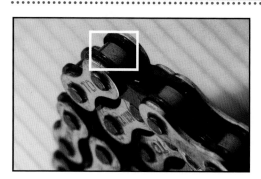

Bicycle-chain link

◆ HUMPTY DUMPTY

Humpty Dumpty sat on a wall;
Humpty Dumpty had a great fall;
All the king's horses
And all the king's men
Couldn't put Humpty Dumpty together again.

Crayons

◆ Zero. After 72 hours it would be midnight again.

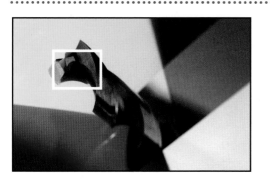

Drill bit

◆ 7 A.D. Since there was no year zero, the transition would have gone from year 1 B.C. to year 1 A.D. Therefore, 11 B.C. to 1 B.C. is ten years, and 1 A.D. to 6 A.D. is six years. Since Octavius waited two more days before applying, the year would have been 7 A.D.

Fish hook or lure

◆ LITTLE MISS MUFFET

Little Miss Muffet
Sat on a tuffet,
Eating her curds and whey;
Along came a spider,
Who sat down beside her
And frightened Miss Muffet away.

Answers for puzzles on pages 44–45

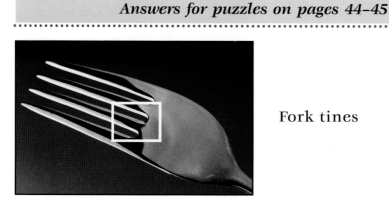

Fork tines

◆ Planting trees. Each seedling encased in the biodegradable container would contain both water and fertilizer. Once dropped from a plane, it would be embedded in the soil by the force of its 198.4 mile (320 km) per hour impact, causing the ruptured case to release its nutrients.

Tree bombing would be capable of planting an acre (0.4 hectare) in minutes whereas an individual planter on the ground would take a week.

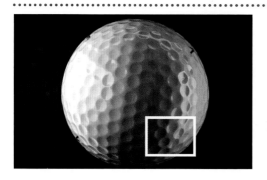

Golf ball

◆ One hundred percent. Since there are more people than there are total hairs on anyone's head, at the very least two people must share the same number of hairs.

■ F.B.I. infiltrators were paying their Communist party membership dues.

A former agent reported in *The Nation* that the F.B.I. had 1,500 infiltrators in the Communist party. That translated into 1 out of every 5.7 party members. The annual dues the numerous informers were paying were funded by the F.B.I., making it the party's largest supporter.

Answers for puzzles on pages 46–47

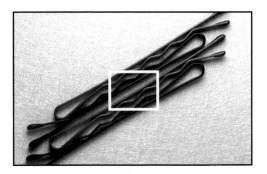

Bobby pins

◆ Never one to lose his cool, Sid quickly removed one lug
nut from each of the other three tires and screwed
them onto the spare.

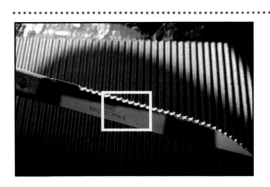

Serrated knife edge

◆ The pickup truck was being transported on one of the
railroad cars.

> *"The louder he talked of honor, the faster we
> counted our spoons."*
>
> Ralph Waldo Emerson (1803–1882)

Answers for puzzles on pages 48–49

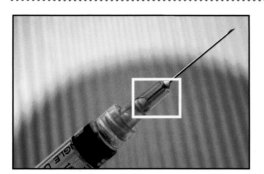

Physician's syringe

◆ WORM. It's the only word which is not the same when spelled backwards.

Vegetable peeler

◆ The oil used to pack them is more expensive by volume than the fish themselves. In actuality, there is no such fish as the sardine. The term *sardine* is actually a generic name for a number of small or immature clupeid fishes. A fish doesn't become a sardine until it has been canned.

■ That's because glass is continuously oozing out of its frame. Glass is actually more liquid than solid, and at room temperature, glass flows like any other liquid. However, because its viscosity is so high, its movement is not apparent. Glass is molecularly a liquid, but with all the properties of a solid except that light can pass through it.

Shoe-polish container

◆ Obviously the pit of lions. If they hadn't eaten in 2 years, they would be quite dead.

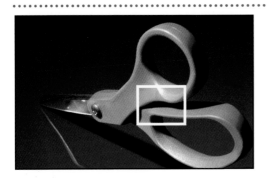

Scissors

◆ A person riding a bicycle.

▪ It's a natural safety device. Many eggs are laid on ledges or surfaces other than a nest. The conical shape makes them roll in a circle, preventing them from rolling away.

Answers for puzzles on pages 52–53

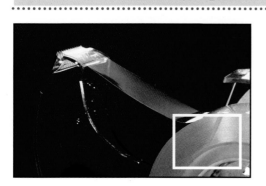

Cellophane tape

◆ The correct answer is F. Incredibly, the pile would rise over 130 million miles (208 million km)!

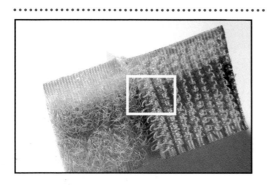

Velcro

◆ This was so that people would take a storm threat seriously. Researchers have found that a warning about Hurricane Claude or Cyclone Amanda will have citizens scurrying for shelter; whereas threats of an anonymous storm, no matter how severe, go practically unheeded.

■ Saturday. Once this tangled question is arranged in the proper sequence, it becomes rather simple. If today is Sunday, what day "precedes the day before yesterday?"— Thursday. Then, "what is the day that follows the day that comes after" Thursday? That's Saturday.

Swiss army knife

◆ Sam's mother.

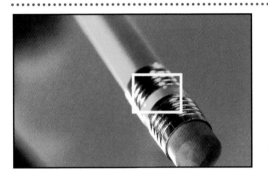

Pencil

◆ This invaluable gift was zero. Before its introduction, simple mathematics such as multiplication, factoring, fractions, and other numerical calculations using the old Roman numeral system were completely impractical. The simple yet ingenious zero is what provides the entire foundation for mathematics, science, engineering, and computer technology.

▓ Barney bought the taxicab for $5,000 and six tires for $600. He put four tires on the car and two in the trunk. After 5,000 miles (8,000 km), he put the front tires on the rear, the rear tires in the trunk, and the trunk tires on the front. After the next 5,000 miles (8,000 km), he put the front tires on the rear, the rear tires in the trunk, and the two trunk tires on the front. At the conclusion of 15,000 miles (8,000 km), each tire will have traveled only 10,000 miles (16,000 km).

Padlock

Tawarik Makutin, who was blind from birth, was the Arab mathematician who invented the zero. He called it "the nothingness that I see encircled by a line."

◆ Art suggested they reduce the size of the reward.

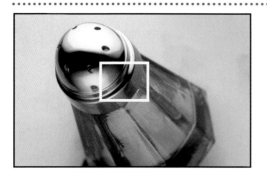

Saltshaker

◆ The year was 1986 B.C. Even 2,000 years ago, the great pyramids were considered an ancient tourist attraction. As long ago as 1986 B.C., some of the great tombs would have been almost 2,000 years old.

Answers for puzzles on pages 58–59

◆ Ned Harper ordered several pairs of dice. The Statistics Department wanted to work with random numbers. Also, the dice would be helpful for the Math Department's study of probability... If in his initial request Ned had asked for two pairs of dice, the college administrators would have flatly refused.

■ None. For cod liver oil, one would have to harvest cod.

> *"LAWSUIT (noun): A machine you go into as a pig and come out of as a sausage."*
>
> Ambrose Bierce (1842–1914)

◆ Jane Barbe is the "time lady." She supplies her voice talent to various companies to announce, "At the tone, the time will be..." Her recorded voice tells the correct time and temperature announcements around the world. AT&T estimates that her records are played more than 25 trillion times per year.

■ Henry was born heir to the throne. After his father died, Henry got the job by succession.

Answers for puzzles on pages 60–61

◆ They were helium balloons.

■ Nothing. The two duelists were really reaching for an excuse to call the whole thing off. After all, when two people are facing each other, they have to be facing in opposite directions.

> *"A verbal contract isn't worth the paper it's written on."*
>
> Samuel Goldwyn
> (1882–1974)

◆ Sam Slug was a blood donor. Being a tad squeamish, when he saw the blood squirting out of his arm, he fainted.

■ Art Bragg. If Art Bragg's statement is true, then either Sam Sham's or Barney Dribble's statement is also true, which cannot be since there is only one true statement. Therefore, if Art Bragg's statement is false, it can only mean that he's the best dancer.

   After all, Beulah may not be the most desirable dance partner, but she knows how to get what she wants.

Answers for puzzles on pages 62–64

◆ One. All the others were coming from the fair.

■ The "Z" would go below the line. All the letters below the line ("B C D E G P T V") rhyme with the letter "Z".

◆ Mr. Greenwich arrived first at 1:45 P.M. He had been told a time that was actually 15 minutes faster than the true time. Ms. Greenwich arrived at 25 minutes after the hour, 2:25 P.M., since she had been told a time that was 25 minutes slower than the true time.

■ The poem is talking about TOMORROW.

◆ Never. Every second cycle the right foot of each will go forward together, but never the left.

■ The word TON.

INDEX to PUZZLE QUESTIONS